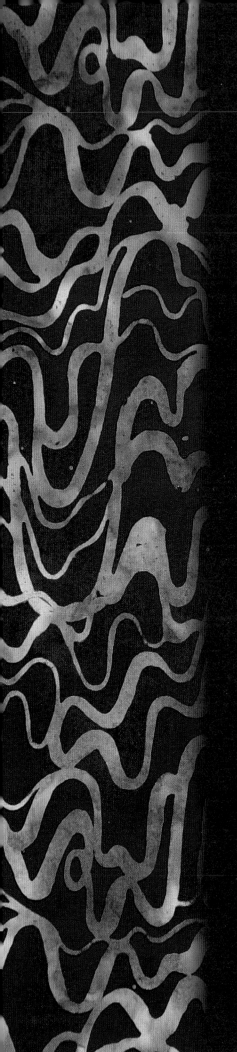

focus on
Batiks

Traditional Quilts in Fun Fabrics

Jan Bode Smiley

C&T PUBLISHING

Text © 2004 Jan Bode Smiley

Artwork © 2004 C&T Publishing

Publisher: Amy Marson

Editorial Director: Gailen Runge

Editor: Cyndy Lyle Rymer

Technical Editors: Sara Kate MacFarland, Karyn Hoyt, and Teresa Stroin

Copyeditor/Proofreader: Eva Simoni Erb

Cover Designer: Kristen Yenche

Design Director/Book Designer: Kristen Yenche

Illustrator: Tim Manibusan

Production Assistant: Kirstie L. McCormick

Photography: Quilt photography by Sharon Risedorph; how-to photography by
Kirstie L. McCormick

Published by C&T Publishing, Inc., P.O. Box 1456, Lafayette, California, 94549

Front cover: *Tulip Garden* by Jan Bode Smiley

Back cover: *Appalachian Spring* by Jan Bode Smiley

Library of Congress Cataloging-in-Publication Data

Smiley, Jan Bode.

    Focus on batiks : traditional quilts in fun fabrics / Jan Bode Smiley.

    p. cm.

Includes bibliographical references and index.

    ISBN 1-57120-230-7 (trade paper)

    1. Quilting—Patterns. 2. Patchwork—Patterns. 3. Batik. I. Title.

    TT835.S5548 2004

    746.46—dc22

                        2003016813

Printed in China

10 9 8 7 6 5 4 3 2 1

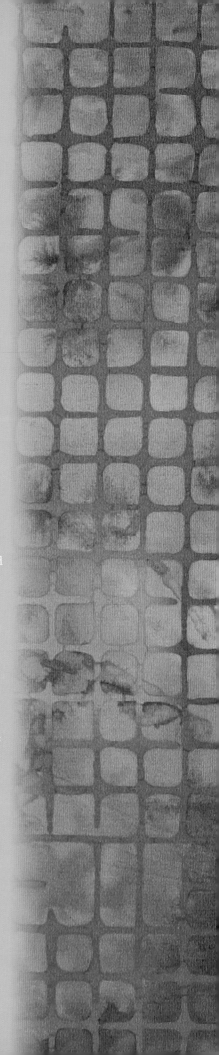

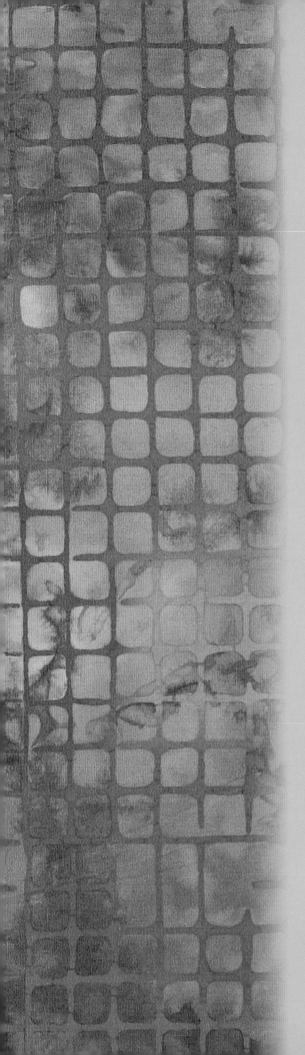

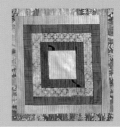

Dedication

To three very special people: My Grandma Bode, who believed that I could do anything. To my Dad, whose presence I still miss, but whose support I feel. For my Mom, who continues to underestimate the strength of her example. Thanks for believing in me.

Acknowledgments

Thanks to Tom, Emma and Keith for their support throughout this process.

Thanks to the wonderful, talented people at C&T who pulled the whole project together and made this book so beautiful. A special thanks to Cyndy for knowing the right things to say when I needed to hear them.

Thanks to everyone who loves batik fabrics — hopefully, as long as we keep buying them, someone will keep making them!

This book would not be what it is without the incredible generosity of the quilt artists whose work appears in the Galleries. Their trust and willingness to share their talent with all of us is truly a gift.

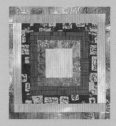

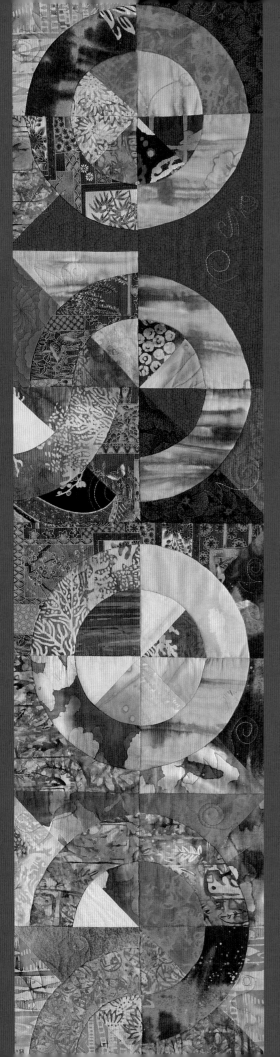

Table of

Contents

Batik Beginnings

In this era of disposable products, I love the fact that we have access to 100 percent handmade fabrics. It is wonderful that we can combine our personal quiltmaking skills with the skills of craftspeople halfway around the world who produce the incredible batik fabrics available today.

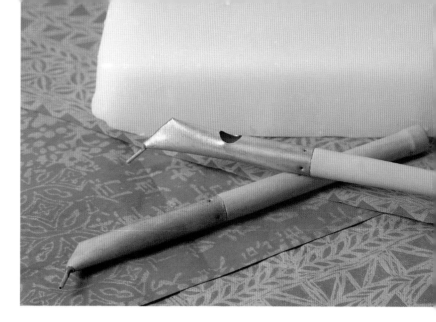

Tjanting tools for drawing a wax design onto cloth

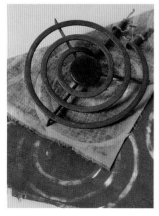

What Is Batik?

Batik is a process of dying fabric. In some languages, the word batik means "to dot" or "wax writing." A pattern is applied to cloth with some type of hot wax or paste. The paste can be made from flour, rice, cassava, or other plant material. After the paste or wax has dried, the fabric is dyed. The areas that have wax or paste on them resist the dye and retain the original color of the cloth. After the dye has been properly set so it will be colorfast, the wax or paste is removed from the cloth.

There are different types of tools designed specifically for applying wax. These include carved wooden blocks and copper tjaps or caps (pronounced chops), which are used to stamp the resist onto the cloth; tjantings or cantings (pronounced chantings) are used to hand draw the resist onto the cloth.

You can also apply wax or paste to cloth using a variety of brushes, metal tools such as a potato masher or metal cookie cutter, wine bottle corks, an old coil from an electric stove, or even something made from inexpensive materials, such as a string block.

TOP TO BOTTOM:
Carved wooden blocks for applying wax, flour, or rice paste to cloth
Copper tjap for applying wax to cloth
Other tools for applying wax to cloth

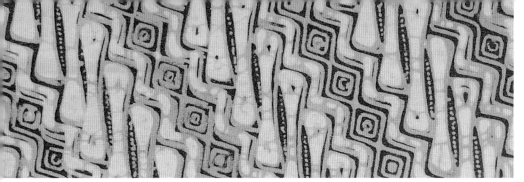

Traditional Indonesian batik

Using a copper tjap to apply wax to cloth on Bali

The fabric is carried outside to dry in the sun on Bali.

Where Do Batik Fabrics Come From?

Batiks are produced in many cultures around the globe, each having its own distinct colors and motifs. Early trade routes supported the exchange of ideas and dyed textiles, influencing the development of batik in other societies. The most common areas of batik production are in Indonesia, Africa, Southeast Asia, and India.

Indonesia

Most of the batik fabrics that we see in quilt shops today are imported from the islands of Java and Bali in Indonesia. Indonesia is a string of over 13,000 islands close to the equator, south of China. Other populations produce resist-dyed clothes, but the Indonesian people honed the craft. Indonesians began to use wax as the resist, and named the process "batik." Traditional Indonesian batik fabrics are produced in earth colors such as soga brown, rust, and creamy white. Originally, only privileged women were allowed to practice the art of batik, but gradually other classes of society were taught the process. Eventually batik fabrics were used for the national costume.

Contemporary Indonesian batik fabrics

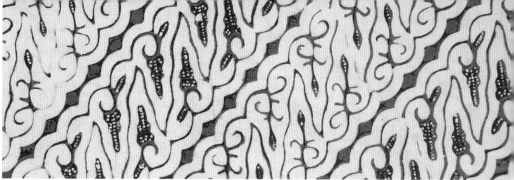

The vast majority of batik fabrics available for consumers today is produced in Indonesia, and bear no resemblance to the traditional batik sarong fabrics worn by the islanders. Contemporary Indonesian batik fabrics made for export now represent the full spectrum of fabrics required for quiltmaking. An incredible variety of colors, patterns, textures, and styles are produced by hand on the islands of Bali and Java, Indonesia.

The wax is boiled off and recycled to be used again.

Fabrics dry in the sun and warm breezes on the island of Bali.
Photos in Bali by Tom Smiley

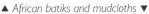
▲ African batiks and mudcloths ▼   Batiks from the collection of Alice Burmeister

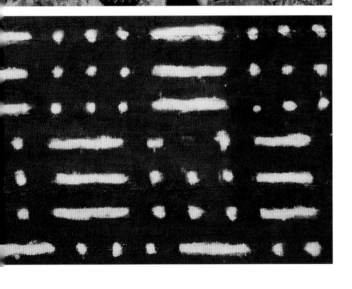

Africa

African batiks are often dyed with traditional natural plant materials, predominantly indigo. Indigo is the oldest dye material used for tradi- tional batik fabrics, and

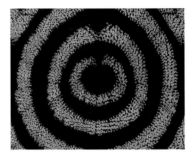
An African indigo-dyed batik

produces the well-known indigo blue and white batiks. Cassava paste is typically used as the resist material for batiks decorated with traditional symbolic motifs. Mudcloth is another form of resist-dyed cloth produced in Africa.

Malaysia

Although batik fabrics have only been produced in Malaysia for three generations, they have already had a significant effect on the region's cultural identity. Located on a peninsula in Southeast Asia, the region has long been an active participant in trade routes. The tropical climate inspires batik motifs of floral bouquets, foliage, and arabesques.

Malaysian batik fabrics

India

Indian batik fabrics are created using carved wooden blocks for stamping the resist onto the cloth; men typically generate the batik. Production of batik fabric for export from India peaked in the seventeenth and eighteenth centuries.

Batik fabric from India

How Long Have People Been Batiking Cloth?

Examples of batik fabrics have been found in the Middle East, India, Central Asia, and the Far East; some cloths have been estimated by scholars to be 2,000 years old. Indonesian cultures have examples of batik dating back to the twelfth century.

Rubber stamp and carved wooden block

Batiks work well in combination with different fabrics.

Unique Properties of Working with Batiks

What are some of the things that make batik fabrics so unique? We've discussed the handmade qualities of batik fabrics, which make them unique in our current high-tech culture. But what else is different about them, and how do they affect us as we work with them?

Reversibility

Remember the previous information on the batik process and the reference to dye baths? When a fabric is submerged in a dye bath, the fabric is dyed all the way through, not just on one side. This results in a different product than fabric that is printed. Screen-printed fabrics are only printed on one side. That's why you see a difference in color between the front and the back of a printed fabric. True batik fabrics don't have a right or a wrong side to them. Sometimes you can determine which side of the fabric the wax was applied to, but usually you can't distinguish one side from the other.

So why is this important? Think about it: the reversibility comes in really handy when you are cutting out fabrics using templates. Since there aren't right or wrong sides, you don't have to worry about mirror-image shapes or sewing the wrong sides together—there are no wrong sides. This is very forgiving for anyone who is "geometrically challenged."

How Can We Make the Most of These Incredible Fabrics?

Batiks are incredibly beautiful fabrics, but don't let them intimidate you. If only batiks are used in a project, the result can sometimes look "muddy". Surrounding them with other fabrics often enhances their beauty. When choosing fabrics for your quilts, try mixing batiks with yarn-dyed woven fabrics, screen prints, and solid hand-dyes. Perhaps you have some fabrics in your "vintage stash" that would be the perfect spark for your next project as you *Focus on Batiks*. The Gallery quilts will also inspire you to incorporate the batik artisan's work in your next quilt project. Let's get started!

Both sides of a batik and a screen-printed fabric

Salt Water Taffy

The inspiration for this quilt was a pieced and appliquéd quilt made by Mrs. Matilda Glish, who resided in northern England; the quilt was dated 1907–14. If you look at just one block, you might think of wrapped candy. If you look at four blocks together you might be reminded of flowers. When viewing the whole quilt, you might think it reminiscent of the Double Wedding Ring pattern. Whichever way you see this pattern, it would make a terrific child's quilt or bright wallhanging for any room. With a softer palette and one of the larger sizes, you will create a wonderful bed quilt. You can appliqué the candy shapes and squares by hand or machine.

Finished Project Sizes

Finished Block Size: 7½" x 7½"

Child-size or Wallhanging-size Quilt: 52" x 52"

Blocks Required: 36 blocks set 6 x 6

Twin-bed Size Quilt: 70" x 85"

Blocks Required: 80 blocks set 8 x 10

Queen-bed Size Quilt: 85" x 100"

Blocks Required: 120 blocks set 10 x 12

Other Supplies

Template plastic

Threads for piecing and quilting

Fusible web

*Note: If you plan to do machine appliqué, remember to add fusible web to the leftover background fabrics before cutting out the candy shapes and the corner squares.

Fabrics You Will Need

	Child/Wallhanging	Twin	Queen
Blocks	½ yard each of 6 fabrics (3 yards total)	1¼ yards each of 6 fabrics (7½ yards total)	1¾ yards each of 6 fabrics (10½ yards total)
Inner border	¼ yard accent fabric	½ yard	½ yard
Outer border	½ yard	1¼ yards	1½ yards
Backing	3¼ yards	5 yards	8½ yards
Batting	56" x 56"	80" x 95"	95" x 110"
Binding	1 yard	1¼ yards	1½ yards

Sufficient yardage provided for wide double binding, to make quilt as shown.

Cutting Instructions
Note: All strips are cut the width of the fabric, from selvage to selvage.

	Child/Wallhanging	Twin	Queen
Background Blocks:	Cut 36 squares 8" x 8".	Cut 80 squares 8" x 8".	Cut 120 squares 8" x 8".
If you are using 6 fabrics	Cut 6 squares of each.	Cut 14 of each.	Cut 20 of each.
Inner border:	Cut 5 strips 1½".	Cut 7 strips 1½".	Cut 9 strips 1½".
Outer border:	Cut 5 strips 3".	Cut 9 strips 4½".	Cut 10 strips 4½".
Binding: [for standard binding]	Cut 6 strips 2¾".	Cut 9 strips 2¾".	Cut 10 strips 2¾".
[for wide double binding]	Cut 6 strips 4¼".	Cut 9 strips 4¼".	Cut 10 strips 4¼".
Appliqué Candy Shapes and Squares*			
If you are using 6 fabrics	Cut 6 candy shapes from each fabric.	Cut 14 candy shapes from each fabric.	Cut 20 candy shapes from each fabric.
	Cut 12 squares 1½" x 1½" from each fabric for the corner squares.	Cut 28 squares 1½" x 1½" from each fabric for corner squares.	Cut 40 squares 1½" x 1½" from each fabric for the corner squares.
If you are using more than 6 fabrics	Cut 36 candy shapes total.	Cut 80 candy shapes total.	Cut 120 candy shapes total.
	Cut 72 squares 1½" x 1½" for the corner squares.	Cut 160 squares 1½" x 1½" for the corner squares.	Cut 240 squares 1½" x 1½" for the corner squares.

Laying Out the Quilt Top

1. Place the number of 8" background squares required for your quilt size on your design wall in a pleasing arrangement, or arrange colors as shown in the photograph.

2. Arrange the appliqué candy shapes and small squares on the background pieces.

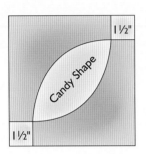

Block layout

Making the Blocks

1. Remove the blocks from your design wall one at a time to avoid confusion.

2. Appliqué the candy shapes and squares onto the background blocks. If you are machine appliquéing, fuse the candy shapes and small squares onto the background blocks, following the manufacturer's instructions for the fusible web you are using.

Putting the Quilt Top Together

1. Sew the blocks into rows, alternating the direction of the seam allowances as you press. This will help make the piecing easier when you sew the rows together.

2. Join the rows together.

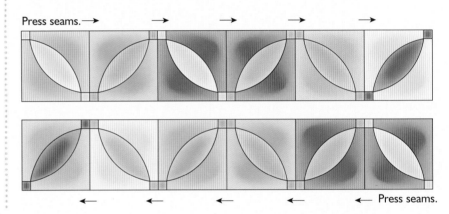

Press seams. →

← Press seams.

Candy Shape Pattern
Add seam allowance if you
are planning to hand appliqué.

Borders and Binding

Refer to page 92 before you piece and cut your borders.

1. Pin, then carefully sew the inner border strips onto the sides of your quilt top. Press.

2. Sew the inner border strips onto the top and bottom. Press.

3. Pin, then carefully sew the outer border strips onto the sides of your quilt top. Press.

4. Sew the outer border strips onto the top and bottom. Press.

Quilting and Finishing

See pages 92–94 for general quilting and finishing instructions.

1. Layer the quilt top, batting, and backing. Pin, thread baste, or use adhesive basting spray.

2. Quilt by hand or machine, using your preferred design, or use the suggested quilting pattern. Several bright colors of thread and a walking foot were used to create meandering diagonal lines across the quilt.

3. Trim the excess batting and backing with a rotary cutter, squaring the quilt as you trim.

4. Bind or finish using your favorite method. *Salt Water Taffy* has a luscious ¾"-wide double bias binding.

Tip

When you are doing a lot of machine quilting, pause periodically and lightly press the quilt to help keep it flat and straight.

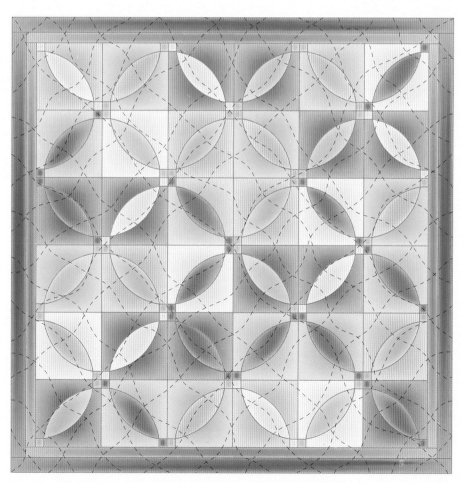

Design suggestion for meandering diagonal quilting

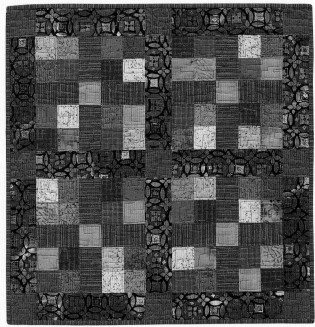

Malaysian
Marketplace

The Malaysian batik panel used for the sashing and borders on all three panels inspired this wonderful triptych. The piecing is simple and quick, with an end result that is deceptively sophisticated.

Finished Quilt Size:
Side panels are each 17" x 31"
Center panel is 31" x 31"

Finished Block Size:
11¼" x 11¼"

Number of Blocks
8
Side panels set 1 x 1
Center panel set 2 x 2 plus sashing

Fabrics You Will Need

1 BATIK PANEL

BRIGHT BATIKS, PLAIDS, STRIPES: 12 assorted fat quarters

PURPLE STRIPE: 1¼ yards for inner block sashing and binding

PURPLE BATIK: ¼ yard for corner blocks

BACKING: 2¼ yards

BATTING: 35" x 35" square for center panel, 2 rectangles 22" x 35" for the side panels

Other Supplies
Threads for piecing and quilting

Cutting Instructions

Panels vary in size. You will need to adjust the sizes of the cut pieces depending on the motif size of the panel you use. Measurements below are for a panel 44" wide by 2½ yards long.

BATIK PANEL: Cut 12 strips 3¼" x 11¾" for the center quilt.

Cut 7 strips 3¼" x 11¾" for each of the smaller side quilts. To add interest, a different section of the batik panel was used for each quilt. You need 26 strips 3¼" x 11¾".

BRIGHTS: Cut 2 strips 2¾" wide from each fat quarter, then cut each strip into 2¾" squares. You need 136 squares.

PURPLE STRIPE: Cut 4 strips 2¾" wide, then cut the strips into 32 rectangles 2¾" x 5" for sashing strips.

PURPLE BATIK: Cut 2 strips 3¼" wide, then cut the strips into 21 squares 3¼" x 3¼" for the sashing corner blocks.

BINDING: Cut 10 strips 2¾" x width of fabric.

Laying Out the Quilt Top
Arrange the double Four-Patch block pieces on your design wall in a manner that pleases you. Stand back and make sure you are spacing your colors nicely.

Tip
If you don't have a large enough room to get a distant viewpoint, try using a reducing glass; or hold a pair of binoculars backwards so you can view the entire quilt top. Polaroid cameras are also good tools for analyzing your quilt in progress.

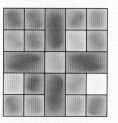

Block layout

Putting the Quilt Top Together

1. Sew the Four-Patch units together.

2. Sew purple sashing strips to the Four-Patch units in the top and bottom rows.

3. Sew the purple sashing to the center square for the middle row.

4. Sew the top and bottom rows to the middle row to complete the block.

5. Press all seam allowances toward the purple sashing strips.

6. Repeat Steps 1–5 to make each panel of the triptych.

7. Arrange the completed blocks on your design wall and place the batik panel strips around every block. Position the 3¼" purple squares at the corners of each block.

8. Sew the blocks and batik panel strips together in sections, alternating the direction of the seam allowances as you press. This will make the piecing easier when you join the sections. Sew the sections together. Repeat these steps for each panel of the triptych.

Quilting and Finishing

See pages 92–94 for general quilting and finishing instructions.

1. Layer the quilt top, batting, and backing. Pin, thread baste, or use adhesive basting spray.

2. Quilt by hand or machine, using your preferred design, or use the suggested quilting pattern. I used a variegated thread that complemented the fabric choices, and free-motion geometric meandering across the blocks and sashing (see photo on page 21).

3. Trim the excess batting and backing with a rotary cutter, squaring the quilt as you trim.

4. Bind or finish using your favorite method.

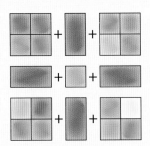

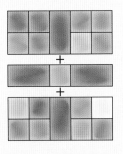

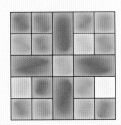

Sew the block together.

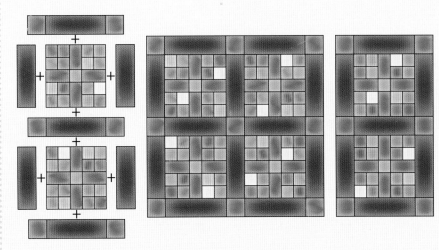

Laying out the quilt top

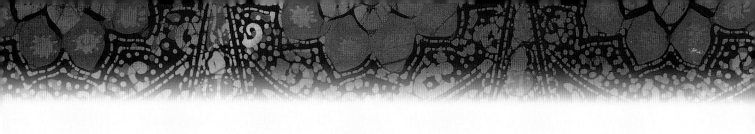

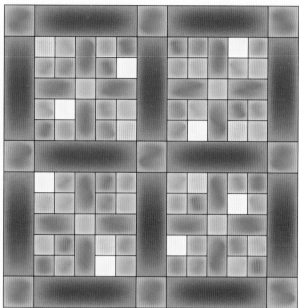

Quilting Diagram

Courthouse Blues

This classic Courthouse Steps layout of the Log Cabin block is fun to sew together, and sure to please. Done in incredibly rich green and blue batiks, it's regal enough for any décor.

Fabrics You Will Need

MEDIUM-LIGHT BATIK: 2 yards for blocks and sashing

DARK BATIK: 2½ yards for blocks and binding

LIGHT: a fat quarter (18" x 22") for the centers of the blocks

BACKING: 3¼ yards

BATTING: 58" x 58"

Other Supplies

Threads for piecing and quilting

Cutting Instructions

MEDIUM-LIGHT BATIK: Cut 25 strips 1½" wide.

From the 25 strips, cut 50 of each length: 1½" x 2", 1½" x 4", 1½" x 6", and 1½" x 8".

Cutting the medium-light batik

Cut 5 strips 2" wide, then from these cut 4 strips 2" x 29" and 8 strips 2" x 10".

DARK BATIK: Cut 35 strips 1½" wide.

From 25 of the strips cut 50 of each length: 1½" x 4", 1½" x 6", and 1½" x 10".

Cut the remaining 10 strips into 50 rectangles 1½" x 8".

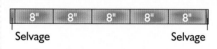
Cutting the dark batik

Cut 4 squares 2" x 2" for the sashing corners. Set aside.

Cut 6 strips 2¾" wide for the binding. Set aside.

LIGHT: Cut 3 strips 2" wide, then cut the strips into 25 squares 2" x 2" for the block centers.

Finished Quilt Size:
50½" x 50½"

Finished Block Size:
9½" x 9½"

Number of Blocks: 25

Blocks Set
5 x 5 plus sashing

Making the Blocks

1. Use a scant ¼" seam allowance throughout the block construction. Sew 2 medium-light batik 1½" x 2" rectangles to opposite sides of the 2" center square. Press.

2. Always press the seam allowances toward the most recently added strips.

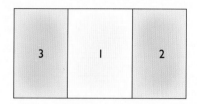
Beginning the block

3. Sew 2 dark batik 4" strips to opposite sides of the unit. Press.

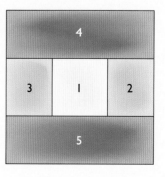
Adding the next strips

4. Sew 2 medium-light batik 4" strips to opposite sides of the unit. Press.

5. Continue adding strips until the block is complete.

Add the next set of strips.

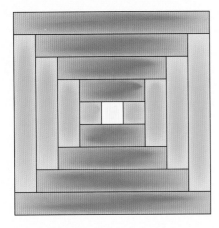

Continue adding strips in the order shown.

Laying Out the Quilt Top

1. Arrange the blocks, sashing strips, and corner blocks on your design wall.

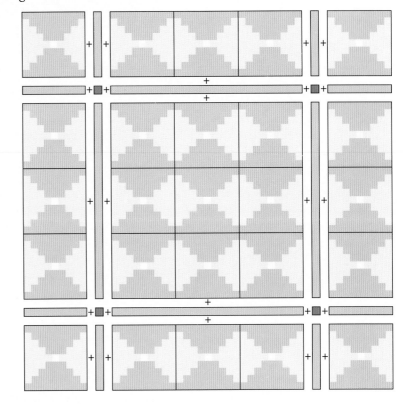

Quilt layout

2. Stand back and make sure you are pleased with your layout.

Putting the Quilt Top Together

1. Sew the 9 center blocks into rows. Press, alternating the direction of the seam allowances. This will help make the piecing easier during the next step. Sew the center section rows together.

2. For each side of the quilt, sew 3 side blocks together.

3. Sew a 29" sashing strip onto each set of side blocks.

4. Sew the side blocks and sashing onto the center section.

5. Sew the top row together, then the bottom row. Sew the remaining sashing strips to the corner blocks, then sew the blocks/sashing strips to the top and bottom rows.

6. Sew the top and bottom rows, with sashing, onto the center section.

Quilting and Finishing

See pages 92–94 for general quilting and finishing instructions.

1. Layer the quilt top, batting, and backing. Pin, thread baste, or use adhesive basting spray.

2. Quilt by hand or machine, using your preferred design, or use the suggested quilting pattern.

3. Trim the excess batting and backing with a rotary cutter, squaring the quilt as you trim.

4. Bind or finish using your favorite method.

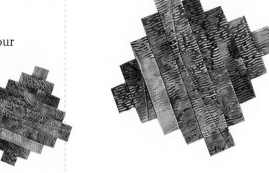

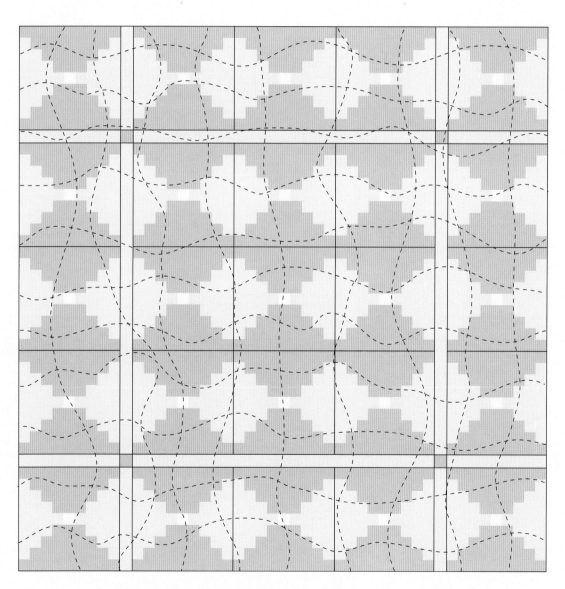

Meandering vertical and horizontal lines create a loose "plaid" quilting design, done with a walking foot and a luscious silk topstitching thread.

CURRENTS

Priscilla Evans Hair, Easley, SC
60" x 42"

Based on the traditional Fair Play design, Priscilla masterfully shaded her fabrics to create this original design with appliquéd cranes.

Gallery Plus offers more options for composing your own quilt with batiks and other fabrics. Each illustration highlights how a major section of the quilt would be constructed.

In *Currents*, the detail was taken from the top-left corner.

Gallery Plus

MOONSCAPE

Joanne Westphal, Chapin, SC
51½" x 67"

Joanne's original design combines piecing and
machine appliqué to complete a quilt begun in
a class with Priscilla Hair.

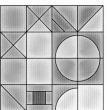

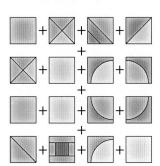

Detail of top-left corner

GALLIMAUFRY

Jan Bode Smiley
68" x 88"

An excessive stash of batik slivers inspired me to the create this strip-pieced quilt top.

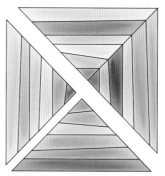

Detail of second and third blocks from
the left in the second and third rows

COLOR NO. 2: BOXED IN

Jan Bode Smiley
52" x 57"

Choosing only a center fabric and the four fabrics that would surround it, I quickly pieced this log cabin quilt and arranged it on the design wall. Adding a strip here and there when sewing the blocks together creates a very fast and fun scrap-based project.

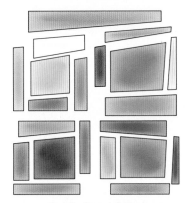

Detail of top-left block

COLOR NO. 6: EMMA'S SQUARES

Jan Bode Smiley
57" x 87"

The traditional Log Cabin block takes on a whole
new look when the same fabric is used for each round
of "logs," creating concentric squares. Batik and hand-dyed
fabrics are perfect for this cheerful quilt for my daughter.

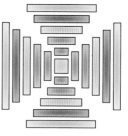

Detail of top-left block

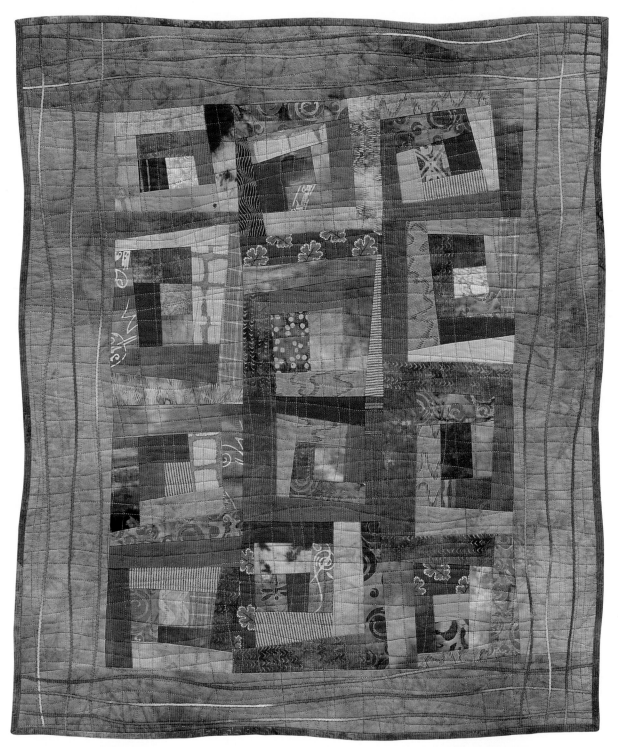

TOAST WITH JAM

Ellen Guerrant, Charlotte, NC
26" x 31"

Machine-pieced free-form Log Cabin blocks take on a rich patina when combined with batik, commercial, recycled, and hand-dyed fabrics. The machine quilting includes some chenille cording.

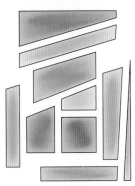

Detail of center block in second row

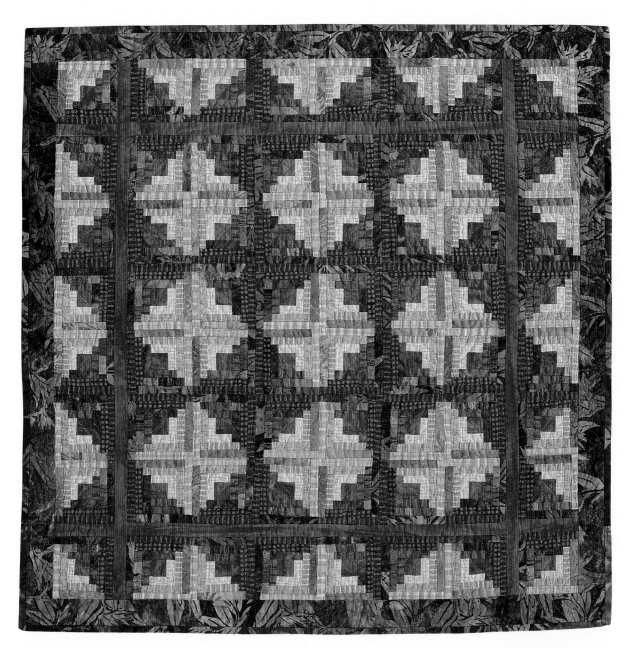

COLOR NO. 4: NEUTRAL LOG CABIN

Jan Bode Smiley
34" x 34"

A classic Log Cabin quilt made from batik and yarn-dyed woven fabrics. Hand quilted in concentric circles.

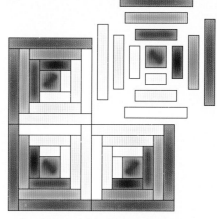

Detail of top-left block, just below sashing

APPALACHIAN SPRING

Jan Bode Smiley
85" x 97", machine quilted by Janice Hayes

Combine two color families, batiks, hand-dyed, and yarn-dyed woven fabrics, and the classic Double Nine-Patch design, and you get a wonderful, warm contemporary quilt. Inspired by the superb spring colors of dogwoods, azaleas, and newly emerging leaf greens.

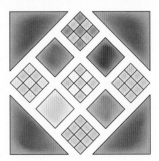

Detail of upper-left corner

SOMEDAY WE WILL LIVE BY THE SEA

Cyndy Lyle Rymer, Danville, CA
40" x 48"

Starting with a gift of the center batik panel, Cyndy was inspired
to create this visual reminder of her goal to save for retirement.

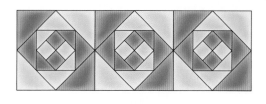 

Details taken from borders at top, right, and left

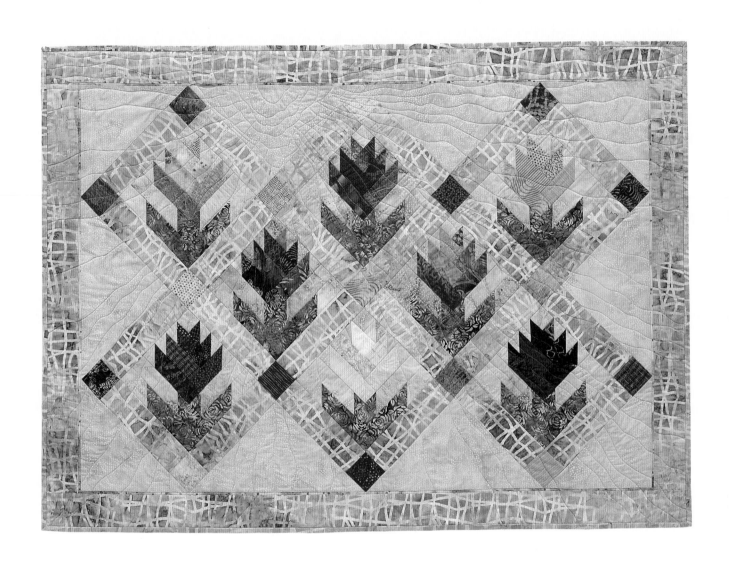

Tulip Garden

*I*magine looking out your window on a beautiful spring morning and seeing the wonderful display of color that can only come from a flower garden. Create this year-round tulip garden based on the Log Cabin block. Using strips and squares, you can easily reproduce these flowers without having to get any dirt under your fingernails. If you're a really ambitious gardener, you can build a paper-pieced picket fence around your tulips. Once completed, this quilt needs no water or fertilizer to continue providing you with a wonderful view from your chair. Armchair gardeners unite!

Finished Quilt Size:
59" x 42"

Finished Block Size: **9"**

Number of Blocks: **8**

Blocks Set On Point

3 x 2 x 3

Fabrics You Will Need

REDS, YELLOWS, PURPLES, AND OTHER COLORS FOR FLOWERS: Scraps of 6 different fabrics from each of 8 color families; minimum size piece: 2" x 2", maximum size: 2" x 6½"

GREEN: ⅜ yard for stems and leaves

ASSORTED BRIGHT FLORALS: 17 squares 3" x 3" for sashing corner blocks

LIGHT BATIK: 1½ yards for block background and side and corner triangles

BRIGHT BATIK: ¼ yard for inner border

PASTEL LATTICE BATIK: 2 yards for sashing strips, outer border, and binding

BACKING: 3½ yards, pieced lengthwise

BATTING: 65" x 50"

Other Supplies

Light-colored thread for piecing

Assorted threads for machine quilting

Cutting Instructions

LIGHT BATIK: Cut 8 strips 2" wide.

From these strips, for each flower block, cut 7 squares 2" x 2", 2 rectangles 2" x 4", and 2 rectangles 2" x 6½".

To make the quilt as shown in the photo, you need a total of 56 squares 2" x 2", 16 rectangles 2" x 4", and 16 rectangles 2" x 6½".

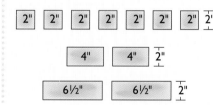

Cutting the background for each block

FLOWER SCRAPS: From each color family, you need 1 square 2" x 2", 2 rectangles 2" x 3½", 2 rectangles 2" x 5", and 1 rectangle 2" x 6½".

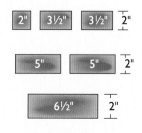

Cutting the flowers

GREEN: Cut 4 strips 2" wide. From these strips, for each block, cut 3 squares 2" x 2", 1 rectangle 2" x 6", and 1 rectangle 2" x 7½".

To make the quilt as shown (8 blocks), you need 24 squares 2" x 2", 8 rectangles 2" x 6", and 8 rectangles 2" x 7½".

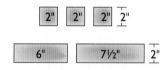

Cutting the stem and leaves for each block

ASSORTED BRIGHT FLORALS: Cut 17 squares 3" x 3" for sashing corner blocks.

LATTICE BATIK: Cut 6 strips 3" wide, from these cut 24 rectangles 3" x 9½" for sashing.

LIGHT BATIK: Cut 2 squares 17½" x 17½" for the side and top and bottom triangles. Cut these in half twice diagonally.

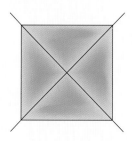

Cutting the side, top, and bottom triangles

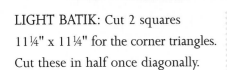

LIGHT BATIK: Cut 2 squares 11¼" x 11¼" for the corner triangles. Cut these in half once diagonally.

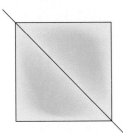

Cutting the corner triangles

BORDERS: Cut 5 strips ¾" wide for the inner border.

Cut 5 strips 3½" wide for the outer border.

BINDING: Cut 6 strips 3" wide.

Making the Blocks

1. Arrange the flower and leaf pieces near your sewing machine.

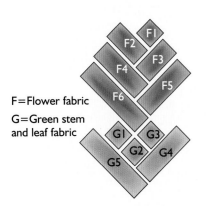

F=Flower fabric
G=Green stem and leaf fabric

Block layout

2. Add the background pieces. With right sides together, place the 2" background squares on the flower fabrics as shown.

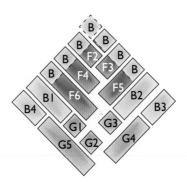

Add the background pieces.

3. Line up 3 outer edges, then stitch on the diagonal of the background square as shown.

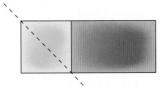

Sew the background square to the flower fabric along the diagonal of the background square.

Note: The background square at the top of the block does not get sewn to anything at this point.

Tip

You can eyeball the diagonal line as you sew, or use a ruler and pencil to mark the diagonal on the wrong side of the background square.

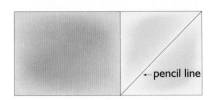

← pencil line

Draw a diagonal line as a sewing guide.

Another option is to fold the square in half on the diagonal and lightly finger-press. Be careful not to stretch the bias if you use this method.

Crease the diagonal.

Note: Always sew on the vertical diagonal. If you have trouble remembering this, use a pin to hold the two pieces together and indicate the direction of your seam.

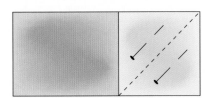

Use pins to help you remember stitching direction.

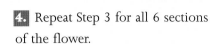

4. Repeat Step 3 for all 6 sections of the flower.

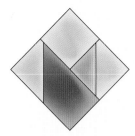

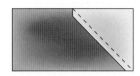

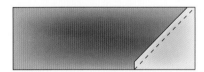

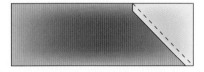

Sew all background squares
to the flower sections.

5. Press each piece flat first, then press the seam allowance toward the flower fabrics.

If you plan to machine quilt, you have the option of leaving the excess fabric attached. If you will be hand quilting, or if you prefer to remove the excess, carefully trim the excess fabric, leaving a ¼" seam allowance.

6. Follow Step 3 to sew the green squares to the background rectangles. Press flat, then press the seam allowance toward the green fabric. Trim the excess seam allowance if you wish.

7. Arrange the background and leaf rectangles as shown. Sew a diagonal line from the upper corner of the leaf fabric to the lower corner of the background rectangle.

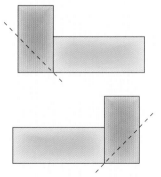

Sew all background squares
to the leaf sections.

Press the excess toward the leaf fabric and trim if desired.

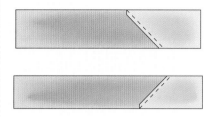

8. Lay out the block next to your sewing machine again, as shown.

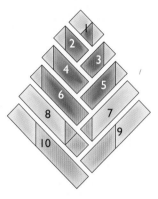

Block ready for assembly

9. Using a scant ¼" seam, start sewing the block together from the top down. First, sew piece 1 to piece 2. Press. Sew this unit to piece 3. Press. Sew this unit to piece 4. Press. Sew this unit to piece 5. Press. Sew this unit to piece 6. Press. Sew this unit to piece 7. Press. Sew this unit to piece 8. Press. Sew this unit piece 9. Press. Sew this unit to piece 10. Press.

10. Repeat this process for each Log Cabin flower block.

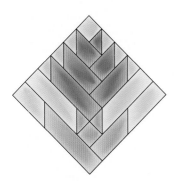

Finished block

Tip

If you don't have a large enough room to view your layout from a distance, try using a reducing glass or hold a pair of binoculars backward to increase your awareness of the whole quilt top. Polaroid cameras are also good tools for analyzing your quilt in progress.

Laying Out the Quilt Top

1. When you are finished making the flower blocks, arrange them on your design wall. Position the 3"-wide sashing strips and 3"-square corner blocks between your pieced flower blocks. Place your side and corner triangles.

2. Stand back and make sure you are pleased with your layout.

Putting the Quilt Top Together

1. Work in diagonal rows, and follow the diagram to sew the quilt top together. Alternate the direction you press the seam allowances for ease in sewing the rows together.

2. Assemble blocks, sashing, sashing blocks, and side triangles first. Add corner triangles to quilt top; then add borders.

Arrange the blocks, sashing and sashing corner blocks, side, and corner triangles.

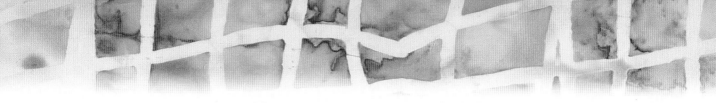

Borders

Refer to page 92 before you piece and cut borders.

1. Sew the ¾"-wide strips for the inner border into one long strip. Cut the lengths needed for the side and top and bottom borders. Sew the side inner border strips to the quilt top, then add the top and bottom inner borders. Press the seams toward the borders.

2. Sew the 3½"-wide strips for the outer border into one long strip. Cut the lengths needed for the side and top and bottom borders. Sew the side outer border strips to the quilt top, then add the top and bottom outer borders. Press seams toward borders.

Quilting and Finishing

See pages 92–94 for general quilting and finishing instructions.

1. Layer the quilt top, batting, and backing. Pin, thread baste, or use adhesive basting spray.

2. Quilt by hand or machine, using your preferred design, or use the quilting suggestion. I used several colors of thread that complemented the fabric choices and machine quilted using a walking foot.

3. Trim the excess batting and backing with a rotary cutter, squaring the quilt as you trim.

4. Bind or finish using your favorite method.

The rays from the warm spring sun are caressing the tulips.

Evening News

I can't look at this quilt without thinking of the newspaper. Is there a better way to relax than with a cup of coffee and the daily paper? If you're not a newspaper reader or crossword puzzle aficionado, don't despair. The black, white, and gray tones are perfect for curling up in front of the television on a cool fall evening to watch the evening news. What a great way to employ those black and white fabrics you've been collecting! Include as many black and white batiks as you can, along with some wonderful black and white screen prints, plaids, and stripes. Don't forget the occasional gray or deepest navy blue that might add just the right spark for your quilt to make the headlines!

Finished Quilt Size:
62¼" x 62¼"

Finished Block Size:
17¼" x 17¼"

Number of Blocks: 9

Blocks Set :
3 x 3 plus sashing

Fabrics You Will Need

BLACK AND WHITE: 1½ yards of one fabric for corner triangles

BLACK AND WHITE: 3 yards of a variety of fabrics for piecing the blocks and corner sashing blocks. Be sure to include an assortment of black backgrounds as well as white backgrounds. Strips can vary from 1" to 3" wide.

SOLID BLACK: 1⅞ yards for the sashing

BACKING: 4 yards

BATTING: 72" x 72"

BINDING: ⅞ yard (A black and white batik was used for the binding on this quilt.)

Other Supplies

Plastic or cardboard template material

Black and white thread for piecing and quilting

Spray starch

Light-weight interfacing, blank newsprint, or extra light-weight fabric for foundation piecing

Cutting Instructions

Cut a 9½" square from cardboard or template plastic, then cut the square in half diagonally. This is your template for the triangles.

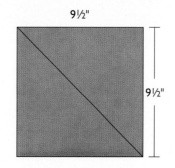

9½"

9½"

Making your template

BLACK AND WHITE FOR CORNER TRIANGLES: Cut 5 strips 9½" wide of your black and white setting fabric. Cut 18 squares 9½" from these strips, then cut the squares in half diagonally. You need 36 black and white triangles.

BLACK AND WHITE FABRICS:
Cut strips varying from 1" to 3" wide. They don't need to be completely straight. Wedge shapes and slightly curved edges can add interest to your pieced triangles.

Irregular strips

For the sake of variety when you are piecing, cut a lot of strips. Cut some strips and piece a few together to determine which fabrics you like best. Cut more fabrics as needed to complete the 36 pieced triangles.

Cut 16 squares 3" x 3" for sashing corner blocks.

SOLID BLACK FABRIC: Cut 12 strips 3" wide. Cut 24 rectangles 3" x 17¾" from these strips.

BINDING: Cut 7 strips 2¾" wide.

Piecing the Triangles

There are several ways to strip-piece these triangles. *Choose the option you are most comfortable with to create 36 pieced triangles.*

OPTION 1: Cut a square approximately 10½" x 10½" from light-weight interfacing, blank newsprint, or lightweight fabric. Cut this square in half diagonally. Using these triangles as your foundation, sew strips of your black and white fabrics to the foundation, using the sew-and-flip technique shown below.

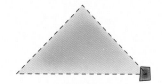

Place a fabric strip right side up over the tip of the foundation triangle.

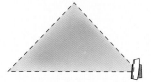

Place a second fabric strip right side down on top of the first strip. Stitch.

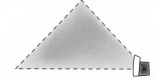

Open up fabric and press. Repeat this process until the foundation is completely covered.

Make sure you completely cover the foundation. After the foundation is completely covered, lightly spray-starch and press your patchwork. Using your cardboard or plastic template, carefully trim the pieced triangle to size.

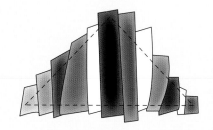

Foundation-pieced triangle

ADVANTAGES OF THIS TECHNIQUE:

Maximum variety of fabric combinations because each triangle is created independently

Foundation will add stability to your off-grain strips.

Can utilize small and odd shape scraps of fabric.

Easy to sew

DISADVANTAGES OF THIS TECHNIQUE:

Because you need to press each strip before adding the next strip, this is not a fast process.

The extra foundation layer, if left in, may result in a bulkier quilt top.

The extra foundation layer, if not left in, will require time and patience to remove.

OPTION 2: Sew your black and white strips together along the long edges, creating a pieced section approximately 14" wide by the entire width of the fabric. Lightly spray starch and press. Use your template to cut triangles; notice the direction of the strips before you cut.

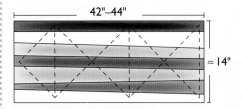

Cutting triangles from crosswise pieced strips

Sew the "leftover" side triangles together along their long side to create a pieced square. From this square, cut two more triangles.

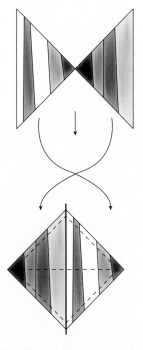

Sew "leftover" sections together.

Note: If your "leftover" pieces are a little small, sew a long strip down the center before joining them together.

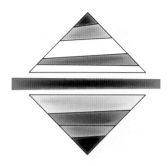

Add another strip in the center if you need to.

ADVANTAGE OF THIS TECHNIQUE:

Quicker than foundation piecing for creating lots of triangles

DISADVANTAGE OF THIS TECHNIQUE:

There is less variety because the fabrics are in the same order in each cut triangle.

Tip

If you don't have a large enough room to view your quilt from a distance, try using a reducing glass, or hold a pair of binoculars backwards to increase your awareness of the whole quilt top. Polaroid cameras are also good tools for analyzing your quilt in progress.

OPTION 3: Cut crosswise strips of your black and white fabrics. Cut the strip into sections approximately 14" wide. Sew these 14" strips together to create a pieced square 14"–15". Lightly starch and press. From the pieced square, cut 2 pieced triangles.

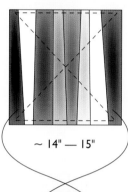

~ 14" — 15"

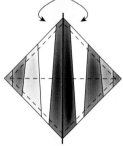

Sew the "leftover" sections together down the center and cut 2 more triangles.

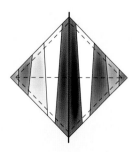

Cut two more triangles.

ADVANTAGES OF THIS TECHNIQUE:

Greater variety of fabric combinations than full-width strip method (Option 2)

Faster than sew-and-flip technique (Option 1)

DISADVANTAGE OF THIS TECHNIQUE:

Slower process than full-width strip method (Option 2)

Laying Out the Quilt Top

Arrange your 36 pieced triangles on your design wall. Position your corner triangles to complete the block layout.

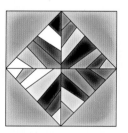

Block layout

Stand back and be sure you are pleased with your layout.

Putting the Quilt Top Together

1. Sew the corner triangles to the adjacent pieced triangles.

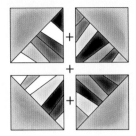

Sew the blocks.

2. Sew the 4 squares together to form each block.

3. Arrange the completed blocks on your design wall. Place your 3" x 17¾" sashing strips between and around the blocks. Arrange the 3" cornerstones at each corner of every block.

4. Referring to the diagram, sew the sashing and the blocks together, alternating the direction of the seam allowances as you press. This will help make the piecing easier during the next step.

5. Sew the rows together to complete the quilt top.

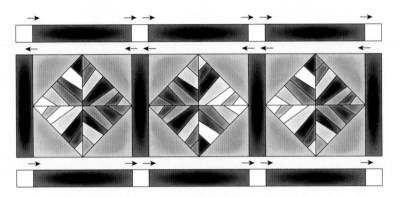

Alternate the direction you press the seams on each row.

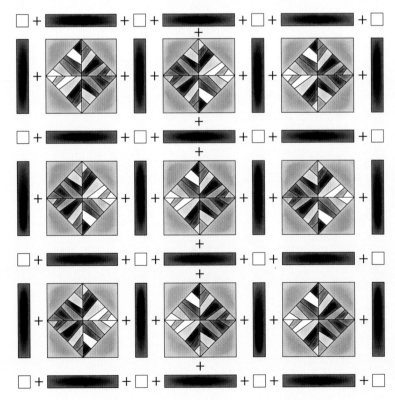

Arranging the sashing, cornerstones, and blocks

Quilting and Finishing

See pages 92–94 for general quilting and finishing instructions.

1. Layer the quilt top, batting, and backing. Pin, thread-baste, or use adhesive basting spray.

2. Quilt by hand or machine using your preferred design, or use the suggested quilting design. *Evening News* was free-motion quilted with black and white thread.

3. Trim the excess batting and backing with a rotary cutter, squaring the quilt as you trim.

4. Bind or finish using your favorite method.

Meandering wavy lines enhance the sashing strips, while free-motion quilting blossoms form the center of each block.

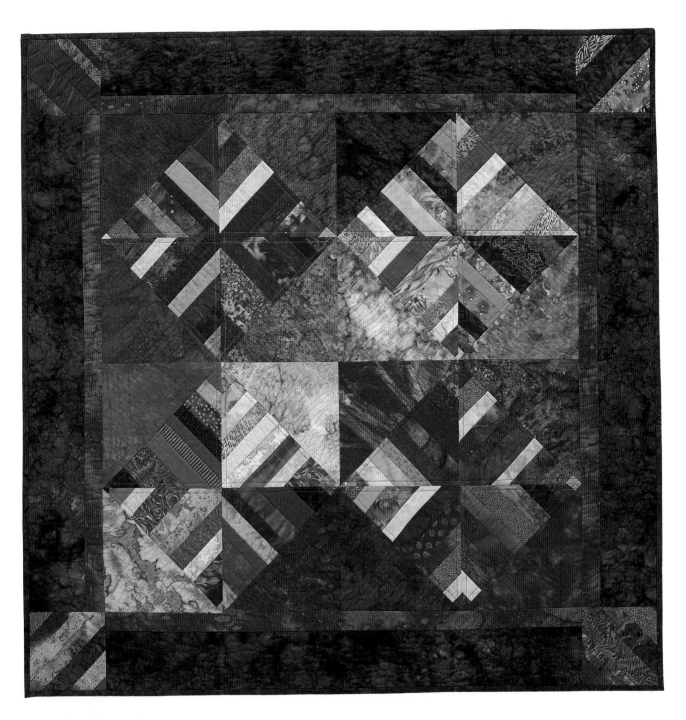

STRING SYMPHONY

Karen G. Wilson, Waxhaw, NC
51" x 51"

Karen chose jewel-tone batiks to create her personal symphony of color after being inspired by the *Evening News* quilt project.

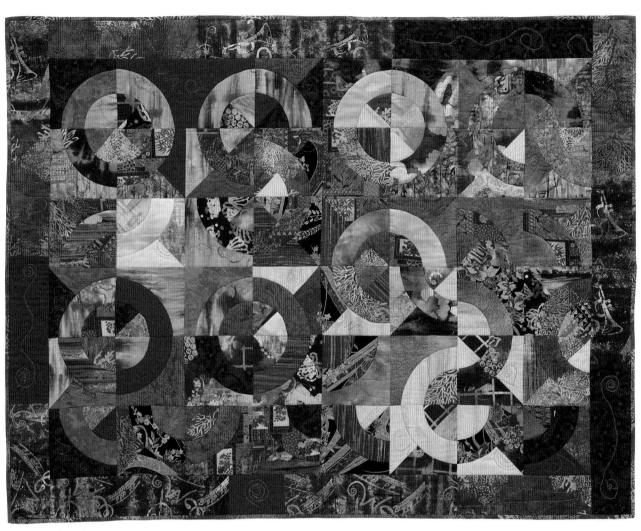

JAZZ

Priscilla Evans Hair, Easley, SC
56" x 44"

This quilt is a wonderful rendition of the traditional pattern called Fair Play.

Gallery 1

FANCY FREE

Kathleen Pappas, Los Angeles, CA
45" x 45"

This 100% batik quilt was designed on the artist's computer. Notice how the corners of the large Star blocks join to form the small Pinwheel blocks.

OCEAN PLAYGROUND

Susan Brittingham, Riner, VA
26" x 27½"

Using batik fabrics and her "upside-down appliqué" technique, the artist created a wonderfully playful quilt incorporating ribbon embellishments and hand beading.

Back

TUTTI FRUTTI

Patricia L. Styring, Jacksonville, FL
79½" x 79½"

Incorporating a traditional Dogtooth Star with original vines and trees done with freezer paper, Patricia succeeded in marrying this challenging combination of colors using batik and other commercial fabrics.

Front

JARRED MEMORY I

Jacquelyn Nouveau, Chapel Hill, NC
42" x 42"

Raw edge appliqué, machine quilting, disperse dying, and organza overlays all combine to create this breathtaking, original quilt.

SEEDS OF SPRING

Nancy Cook, Charlotte, NC
20" x 23"

A cluster of deep maroon maple seeds on Nancy's garden path inspired this small and lovely pieced quilt. This quilt was partially completed in a workshop taught by Ruth McDowell.

GINKGO

Carol Vasenko, Newark, OH
25¾" x 32¼"

Using commercial batiks along with hand-dyed fabrics,
Carol pieced the quilt top before creating the free-motion
embroidered ginkgo leaves.

INNER POWER

Martine House, Columbus, NC
12" wide x 25" high x 2" deep

Inspired by the batik fabric designed by Carol and Marty Britt, Martine experimented with hand-dyed and handmade silk paper. On the front of the paper, Martine enhanced her original creation with intricate, sculptural peyote-stitch beadwork.

ESCAPE

Jan Bode Smiley
48" x 45"

This exuberant quilt grew out of an exercise, given by Nancy Crow, in curved and strip piecing.

15 Bean Soup

Recipe for Bean Soup

1. Find an earth-tone batik fabric you absolutely love. Buy 4 yards of it.

2. Gather together a generous helping of complementary colors. Just a pinch of each fabric will do (5" x 10" scraps).

3. Mix the fabrics together so the colors thoroughly enhance one another. Allow them to rest for at least one hour, more time if you prefer.

4. Look again at your mixture of fabrics with a fresh eye. Decide which flavors/colors you like best with your main fabric, and with one another. For this recipe, I used three different color families: purple, rust-gold, and green.

5. From each of your color groups, select a variety of values and textures. To spice up your quilt, be sure to mix light, medium, and dark values and vary the scale of the prints. This sample quilt mixed together 12–16 different fabrics of each color family. This is a great project for including scraps of screen prints, plaids, batiks, and both old and new fabrics.

6. Follow the cutting and sewing recipe that follows.

Fabrics You Will Need

EARTH-TONE BATIK: 4 yards for blocks, outer border, and binding

ACCENTS: 2 yards total; minimum scrap size 5" x 10"

MEDIUM ACCENT: ⅓ yard for inner border

BACKING: 5 yards

BATTING: 64" x 80"

Other Supplies
Threads for piecing and quilting

Cutting Instructions

EARTH-TONE BATIK: Cut 6 strips 4⅞" wide. Cut each strip into 8 squares 4⅞" x 4⅞", then cut the squares in half diagonally. You need 96 triangles of the main fabric.

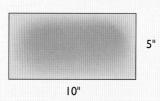

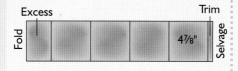

Cutting triangles
Cut squares in half diagonally.

Cut 12 strips 2½" wide. Cut 16 squares 2½" x 2½" from each strip. You need 192 of the 2½" squares.

Finished Quilt Size:
59" x 75"

Finished Block Size:
8" x 8"

Number of Blocks:
48

Blocks Set :
6 x 8

ACCENTS: Cut a 10" x 5" rectangle of each of your accent fabrics. From this rectangle, cut a 5" x 5" square. Cut the square in half vertically and then in half horizontally to yield 4 squares 2½" x 2½". From the left-over piece, cut a 4⅞" x 4⅞" square, then cut the square in half diagonally to yield 2 triangles. You need 192 of the 2½" x 2½" squares of accent fabrics, and 96 triangles of the accent fabrics.

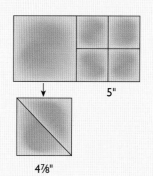

Cutting accent fabrics: cut 4 squares 2½" x 2½", cut 1 square 5" x 5"; trim to 4⅞", then cut diagonally.

Tip

Cut more than the needed number of squares and triangles from your accent fabrics to give you flexibility when you are laying out the quilt top.

INNER BORDER: From medium accent fabric cut 6 strips 1¼" wide.

OUTER BORDER: Cut 7 strips 5" wide.

BINDING: Cut 8 strips 2¾" wide.

Laying Out the Quilt Top

1. Arrange the quilt block pieces on your design wall. Stand back and make sure you are spacing your colors, textures, and print scales nicely.

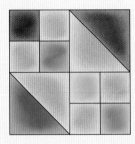

Block layout

2. When laying out the whole quilt, make sure you orient the triangles in each block the correct way.

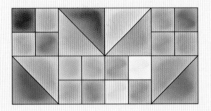

Quilt layout

Making the Blocks

1. Sew the Four-Patch units together.

2. Sew the triangles together.

3. Sew the Four-Patches to the triangles to complete each block unit.

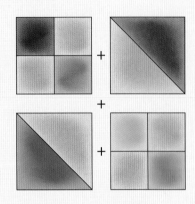

Sew the block together.

Tip

If you don't have a large enough room to view your quilt from a distance, try using a reducing glass or hold a pair of binoculars backwards to increase your awareness of the whole quilt top. Polaroid cameras are also good tools for analyzing your quilt in progress.

Putting the Quilt Top Together

1. Sew the blocks into rows, alternating the direction of the seam allowances as you press. This will make the next step easier.

2. Join the rows together.

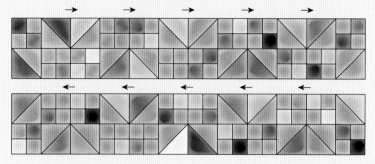

Alternate the direction you press the seams on each row.

Borders and Binding

1. Refer to page 92 before you piece and cut your borders.

2. Add the side border strips to the quilt top, then add the top and bottom borders. Press the seams toward the borders.

Quilting and Finishing

See pages 92–94 for general quilting and finishing instructions.

1. Layer the quilt top, batting, and backing. Pin, thread-baste, or use adhesive basting spray.

2. Quilt by hand or machine using the design shown below, or your own quilting pattern. I used a walking foot to meander-quilt lines in several colors of thread diagonally across the quilt blocks.

3. Trim the excess batting and backing with a rotary cutter, squaring the quilt as you trim.

4. Bind or finish using your favorite method.

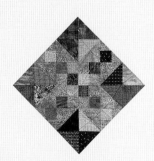

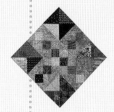

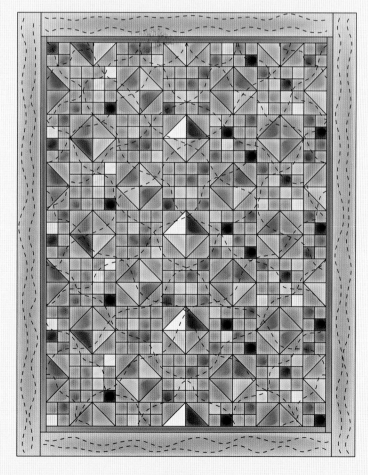

Quilting diagram

Cosmic Carousel

Can you imagine how much fun it would be to ride on a carousel with a view of the entire galaxy? Bright, swirling colors and simple shapes combine to create this wonderful quilt. If the bright colors are too much for you, don't be discouraged. This pattern also looks terrific as a simple two-color quilt. Strap on your seatbelt and grab some of your favorite batiks. It's time for this ride to begin!

Finished Quilt Size:
52½" x 52½"

Finished Block Size:
10" x 10"

Number of Blocks: 16

Blocks Set:
4 x 4 plus a pieced border

Fabrics You Will Need

NAVY DOT: 1½ yards for blocks and pieced border

BRIGHTS: 1½ yards total of assorted brights (orange, fuchsia, mango) for blocks and pieced border Minimum piece size 18" x 6" (*Cosmic Carousel* was made with 12 different bright fabrics.)

NAVY BLUE: ½ yard for the pieced border

BRIGHT ACCENT: ½ yard for the outer border

BACKING: 3¼ yards

BATTING: 57½" x 57½"

BINDING: ⅝ yard

Other Supplies

A 6" or 8" square acrylic ruler is very helpful when cutting the pieces for this quilt.

Threads for piecing and quilting

Cutting Instructions

NAVY DOT: Cut 3 strips 5⅞" wide. Cut 16 squares 5⅞" x 5⅞" from these strips, then cut the squares in half diagonally. You need 32 large triangles of the navy dot.

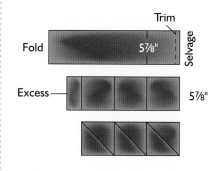

Cutting triangles

Cut 2 strips 4⅜" wide. Cut 16 squares 4⅜" x 4⅜" from the strips, then cut the squares in half diagonally. You need 32 medium triangles of navy dot.

Cut 2 strips 3⅜" wide. Cut 16 squares 3⅜" x 3⅜" from the strips, then cut the squares in half diagonally. You need 32 small triangles of navy dot.

Cut 2 strips 2¼" wide, then cut the strips into 32 squares 2¼" x 2¼".

Cut 2 strips 5⅞" wide. Cut 10 squares 5⅞" x 5⅞", then cut the squares in half diagonally. You need 20 triangles for the pieced border.

ASSORTED BRIGHTS: Cut 16 squares 5⅞" x 5⅞", then cut the squares in half diagonally. You need 32 bright large triangles.

Cut 16 squares 4⅜" x 4⅜", then cut the squares in half diagonally. You need 32 bright medium triangles.

Cut 16 squares 3⅜" x 3⅜", then cut the squares in half diagonally. You need 32 bright small triangles.

Cut 32 squares 2¼" x 2¼".

Tip

Cut more than the needed number of squares and triangles from your bright fabrics to give you flexibility when you are laying out the quilt top.

From your bright fabrics, cut 8 squares 5⅞" x 5⅞", then cut the squares in half diagonally. You need 16 triangles for the pieced border.

NAVY BLUE: Cut 3 strips 5⅞" wide. Cut 18 squares 5⅞" x 5⅞", then cut the squares in half diagonally. You need 36 triangles.

OUTER BORDER: Cut 6 strips 2" wide x the width of the fabric from one of your bright fabrics.

BINDING: Cut 6 strips 2¾" wide x the width of the fabric.

Laying Out the Quilt Top

1. For this quilt, all of the parts of the blocks are laid out before you sew them together. On your design wall, arrange the navy dot to create the spiraling pattern that is evident when the blocks are repeated. Notice that the position of the navy dot alternates between blocks.

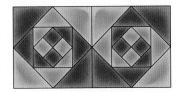

Block layout

2. Use your bright fabrics to fill in the rest of the blocks. Randomly place your various bright fabrics in a pleasing arrangement. Stand back and make sure you are spacing your bright fabrics nicely.

Tip

When adding the triangles, center them on the unit to which they will be sewn. There are two reference points you can use. One way to check is to be sure that an equal amount of the "dog-eared" triangles extend beyond the piece. The other is that the center of the triangle should intersect a previous seam line. Using care when positioning your triangle units will help you achieve square finished blocks.

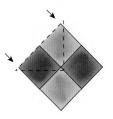

Centering the triangles

Making the Blocks

1. Sew the center Four-Patch units, alternating seam allowances when pressing. Press the completed Four-Patch units.

2. Sew the 2 bright small triangles onto opposite sides of the Four-Patch unit, referring to the quilt block layout. Always press toward the most recently added triangles.

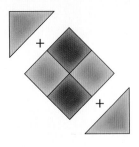

3. Sew the 2 navy dot small triangles onto opposite sides.

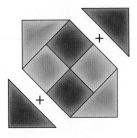

4. Sew the 2 bright medium triangles onto opposite sides.

5. Sew the 2 navy dot medium triangles onto opposite sides.

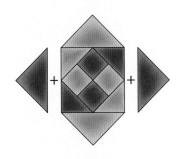

Sewing the blocks

6. Sew the 2 bright large triangles onto opposite sides. Sew the 2 navy dot triangles onto opposite sides.

7. Repeat Steps 1–6 until you have 16 blocks.

When you are happy with the arrangement of your blocks, stand back and verify that the spiral is moving in the same direction all over the quilt.

Tip

If you don't have a large enough room to view the layout from a distance, try using a reducing glass, or hold a pair of binoculars backwards to increase your awareness of the whole quilt top. Polaroid cameras are also good tools for analyzing your quilt in progress.

Putting the Quilt Top Together

1. Sew the blocks into rows, alternating the direction of the seam allowances as you press. This will help make the next step easier.

2. Piece the rows together.

Making the Pieced Border

1. With your 16-block unit sewn together, you are ready to make the pieced border. Arrange the navy dot triangles, the navy background fabric triangles, and the bright triangles around the perimeter of your blocks. Be sure you position the triangles to complete the design radiating from the blocks. Refer to the color photograph of the finished quilt.

2. Piece the triangle units into squares. Piece the squares together to form the border sections.

3. Sew the side borders to the quilt top. Add the upper and lower borders.

Borders and Binding

Refer to page 92 before you piece and cut the borders.

Quilting and Finishing

See pages 92–94 for general quilting and finishing instructions.

1. Layer the quilt top, batting, and backing. Pin, thread baste, or use adhesive basting spray.

2. Quilt by hand or machine, using your preferred design, or use the quilting suggestion. I used both mango and navy quilting threads.

3. Trim the excess batting and backing with a rotary cutter, squaring the quilt as you trim.

4. Bind or finish using your favorite method.

Piecing the borders

Free-motion quilting emphasizes the spiraling motion of the carousel.

Maltese
Reflections

Claire Tinsley designed this Malta-inspired quilt to remind her of the hot, dry land surrounded by the Mediterranean. She foundation pieced the quilt with an emphasis on batik fabrics.

Finished Quilt Size:
40½" x 63½"

Finished Block Size:
4½" x 4½"

Number of Blocks: 140

Block Set: 10 x 14

Fabrics You Will Need

Note: The cutting instructions given are exact. If you are a beginner, you may want to purchase extra fabric.

BRIGHT ORANGE: 1 yard

ORANGE AND BLUE PRINT: 2⅛ yards each

MULTICOLORED: 1¼ yards

INDIGO: 2 yards

LIGHT BLUE: 1 yard

LIGHT YELLOW: 1⅜ yards

DARK ORANGE: ⅝ yard

BACKING: 55" x 75"

BATTING: 55" x 75"

BINDING: ⅝ yard

Other Supplies

Threads to match for piecing and quilting

Cutting Instructions

Note: The sizes given are exact. If you are a beginner, you may want to cut larger pieces.

BRIGHT ORANGE: Cut 3 strips 6" wide, then cut the strips into 24 rectangles 6" x 4".

Cut 3 strips 4½" wide, then cut the strips into 48 rectangles 4½" x 2½".

ORANGE AND BLUE PRINT: Cut 8 strips 1¾" wide, then cut the strips into 48 rectangles 1¾" x 6".

Cut 6 strips 4½" wide, then cut the strips into 96 rectangles 4½" x 2½".

BINDING: Cut 7 strips 2¾" wide x width of fabric.

MULTICOLORED: Cut 9 strips 4½" wide, then cut the strips into 136 rectangles 4½" x 2½".

INDIGO: Cut 5 strips 8" wide, then cut the strips into 44 rectangles 8" x 4".

Cut 5 strips 6" wide, then cut the strips into 48 rectangles 6" x 4".

LIGHT BLUE: Cut 15 strips 1¾" wide, then cut the strips into 96 rectangles 1¾" x 6".

LIGHT YELLOW: Cut 6 strips 4½" wide, then cut the strips into 96 rectangles 4½" x 2½".

Cut 3 strips 6" wide, then cut the strips into 24 rectangles 6" x 4".

DARK ORANGE: Cut 8 strips 1¾" wide, then cut the strips into 48 rectangles 1¾" x 6".

Making the Blocks

Refer to Quilting Basics, page 94, for paper piecing instructions.

Make 96 copies of the foundation template for Blocks A, B, C, and D on page 68.

Make 40 copies of the foundation template for the border and 4 copies for the corner blocks on page 69.

Block A

1. Place a 6" x 4" bright orange rectangle on the non-printed side of the paper, making sure to completely cover section 1. Pin in place. Trim to a ¼" seam allowance.

2. Align a 1¾" x 6" orange and blue print rectangle with the long edge of piece 1, right sides together, and pin. Stitch the seam. Open and press to cover section 2. Trim to a ¼" seam allowance.

3. Repeat Step 2 for section 3.

4. Align a 4½" x 2½" multicolored rectangle with the edge of piece 2, right sides together, and pin. Stitch the seam. Open and press to cover section 4.

5. Align a 4½" x 2½" multicolored rectangle with the edge of piece 3, right sides together, and pin. Stitch the seam. Open and press to cover section 5.

6. Align a 4½" x 2½" bright orange rectangle with the short edge of piece 1, right sides together, and pin. Stitch the seam. Open and press to cover section 6. Trim the block to a ¼" seam allowance.

7. Make 24.

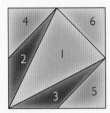

Block A
Make 24.

Block B

Repeat Steps 1–6 of block A using the following colors.

Section 1: indigo

Sections 2 and 3: light blue

Section 4: multicolored

Section 5: light yellow

Section 6: orange and blue print

Make 24.

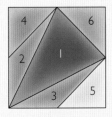

Block B
Make 24.

Block C

Repeat Steps 1–6 of block A. These blocks should mirror block B.

Section 1: indigo

Sections 2 and 3: light blue

Section 4: light yellow

Section 5: multicolored

Section 6: orange and blue print

Make 24.

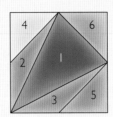

Block C
Make 24.

Block D

Repeat Steps 1–6 of block A using the following colors.

Section 1: light yellow

Sections 2 and 3: dark orange

Sections 4 and 5: light yellow

Section 6: bright orange

Make 24.

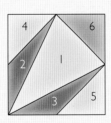

Block D
Make 24.

Making the Border Blocks

1. Place an 8" x 4" indigo rectangle on the non-printed side of the paper, making sure to completely cover section 1. Pin in place. Trim to a ¼" seam allowance.

2. Align a 4½" x 2½" multicolor rectangle with the long edge of piece 1, right sides together, and pin. Stitch the seam. Open and press to cover section 2.

3. Align a 4½" x 2½" orange and blue print rectangle with the long edge of piece 1, right sides together, and pin. Stitch the seam. Open and press to cover section 3. Trim the block to a ¼" seam allowance.

Make 40.

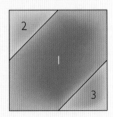

Border Block
Make 40.

Making the Corner Blocks

Repeat Steps 1–3 of Making the Border Blocks using the following colors.

Section 1: indigo

Sections 2 and 3: orange and blue print

Make 4.

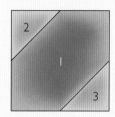

Corner Block, Make 4.

When all blocks are completed, remove paper foundations.

Laying Out the Quilt Top

Arrange the blocks on your design wall using the photo of the quilt as a guide.

Putting the Quilt Top Together

1. Place the first two blocks right sides together and pin, matching corners and angles. This will enable you to get accurate piecing. Stitch along the seamline. Continue sewing the blocks into pairs.

2. Sew the pairs into rows, alternating the direction of the seam allowance as you press each row.

3. Sew the rows together.

Quilting and Finishing

See pages 92–94 for general quilting and finishing instructions.

1. Layer the quilt top, batting, and backing. Pin, thread baste, or use adhesive basting spray.

2. Quilt by hand or machine using your preferred design.

3. Trim the excess batting and backing with a rotary cutter, squaring the quilt as you trim.

4. Bind or finish using your favorite method.

Quilt Layout

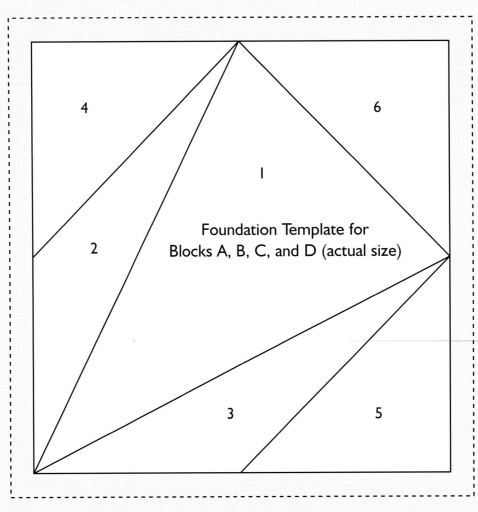

4

6

I

2

Foundation Template for
Blocks A, B, C, and D (actual size)

3

5

5" x 5"

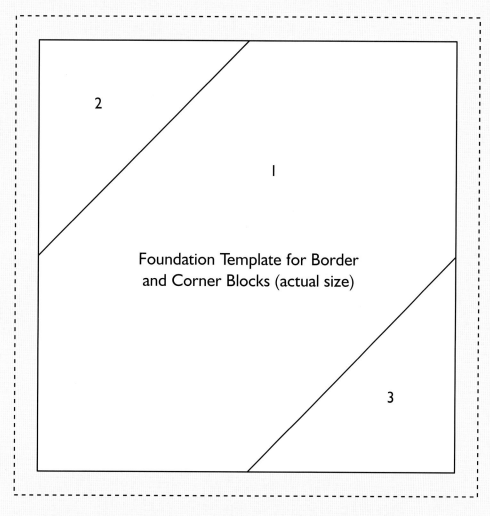

Foundation Template for Border
and Corner Blocks (actual size)

5" x 5"

Detail from Ichiban, *Jan Bode Smiley*, 32" x 28½"

Batik your Own Fabric

How to Make Your Own Batik Fabric

Despite the abundance of batiks available today, you may be tempted to create your own fabrics. Here's a wonderful opportunity to design your own batik fabric on a small scale. You can play with dyes or paints and some resist, which is traditionally hot wax or paste, but now can be made as a cold-water solution. I will lead you through the process; just read all of the text to be sure you have the necessary supplies **before** you get started.

Fabrics You Will Need

Assorted hand-dyed fabrics, solid-colored commercial fabric, Bali hand-painted fabric, or plain cotton muslin

Other Supplies

Procion dyes or acrylic paints

Dye thickener

Dye activator or soda ash

Measuring cup and spoons
(never to be used for food again)

Cold water wax solution or other water-based resist

Synthrapol

Foam brushes

Small containers for mixing dyes
(disposable containers are great!)

Plastic to protect your work surface

Clean paper grocery bags or newspaper*

*Note: If you are using newspaper, don't use the current paper. In order to prevent the newsprint from transferring to your cloth, the papers should be about 2 weeks old.

Iron

Rotary cutter, ruler, and mat

Threads for piecing and quilting

Optional items for applying the resist:

Wood block approximately 4" x 6"
(or a size to fit your desired design)

³⁄₁₆" cotton clothesline

Glue**

**Note: If you are using a water-based white glue such as Sobo or Elmer's, take care not to expose the finished block to a lot of water.

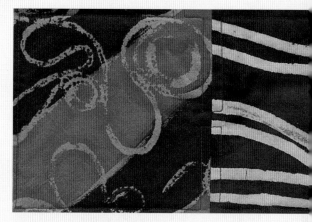

Detail from Jungle Fever *(page 75)*

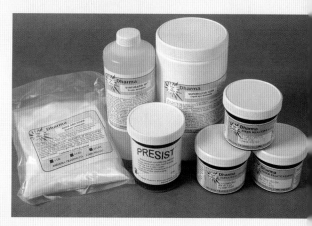

Tip
An inexpensive flannel-backed vinyl tablecloth offers great protection and is reusable.

Found Objects
Use your imagination or any of the following items to make great patterns on fabric.

Celery, carved potatoes, or other vegetables

The sole of an old shoe

Potato masher

Old oven coil

Carved linoleum block

Wine bottle cork

Foam cut into shapes and glued to wood or acrylic block

Purchased foam or rubber stamps

Sources: Check the source listings in the back of the book for suppliers of dye products.

Batik Instructions

Making a String Block

1. Spread glue on the bottom of a wood block.

2. Arrange the cotton clothesline or string in an interesting pattern.

Homemade string blocks

3. Allow the glue to dry for at least 2 hours.

4. Your block is now ready to use.

Read all the safety information on your dye products. Arrange a workspace away from food preparation areas. Protect your work surface with plastic.

Applying the Design to Your Fabric

1. Using the foam brush, apply the cold-water wax solution or other resist of your choice to the pattern on your wood block. Press the block onto the fabric. Repeat to create your design in regular or irregular patterns.

2. Allow the resist to dry completely. Depending on humidity and temperature, this may take 2–3 hours. Be sure the solution is completely dry before going on to the next step.

Adding Color With Fabric Dyes

Prepare your dye solution for painting on the color.

1. Prepare 4 cups of dye thickener according to the manufacturer's instructions, or use commercially prepared dye thickener.

2. Measure out 1 cup of solution, then divide the remaining amount into 6 parts of ½ cup each.

3. Add 1 to 1½ teaspoons of dye powder to each of the 6 containers containing ½ cup dye thickener. To the 1 cup of solution, add 2 to 2½ teaspoons of dye powder. This is for a piece of fabric large enough to be used as the focal fabric in a quilt, or to cut into borders.

4. Immediately prior to using each color, add ¼ teaspoon dye activator.

5. Brush this solution all over the fabric.

Repeat this process with each of your desired colors.

6. Allow the dye-painted fabric to air dry and cure for 24 hours.

Follow the manufacturer's instructions on your resist product to remove the resist from your fabric.

7. To remove excess dye, rinse your fabric in hot water. After several rinses, wash the fabric with Synthrapol, following the manufacturer's instructions, until the rinse water is clear.

8. Your fabric is now ready to cut and sew into your quilt.

Tip

Be sure to test your resist on a small piece of cloth before you attempt a large piece. The resist will more easily penetrate a smooth, high-thread-count fabric than a thick, textured fabric.

Loofah and twigs

Wire grid fasteners, cork and makeup sponges

Pasta shapes shown with wax brick

Adding Color With Acrylic Paints

1. Pour or scoop acrylic paint into your disposable container.

2. Add water to thin the paint to a consistency similar to warm honey.

3. Brush the thinned acrylic paint all over the fabric.

Repeat this process with each of your desired colors.

4. Allow the painted fabric to air dry and cure for 24 hours. Follow the manufacturer's instructions on your paints to ensure that they will be colorfast. Paints that require heat setting will need to be set before rinsing.

5. Follow the manufacturer's instructions on your resist product to remove the resist from your fabric.

6. Rinse your fabric in hot water until the rinse water is clear. Wash the fabric with any detergent.

7. Your fabric is now ready to cut and sew into your quilt.

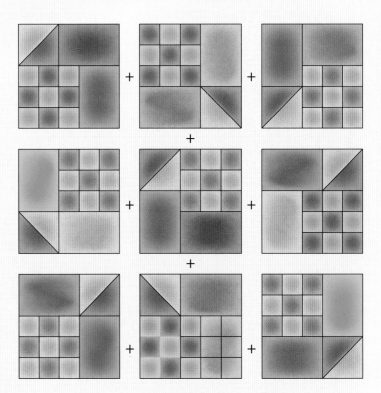

Diagram for making a quilt like *Rhyme or Reason*.

RHYME OR REASON

Susan Webb Lee, Weddington, NC
37½" x 37½"
All hand-dyed and hand-batiked fabric

JUNGLE FEVER

Susan Webb Lee, Weddington, NC
31" x 40"

Hand-dyed and hand-batiked fabrics
mixed with commercial batik and
striped fabrics

DOOR #1: WHY

Jan Bode Smiley
33" x 73"

The door panels were stamped with hand carved stamps. "Planks" of batik fabric surround these panels to create this life-size fabric door.

KALEIDOSCOPIC XXI: THE THANK YOUR LUCKY STARS MEMORIAL QUILT

Paula Nadelstern, The Bronx, New York City
40" x 40", cotton and silk

To its maker, every quilt becomes a soft document, chronicling the events that took place during its evolution. In this case, what began as a requiem for one family member turned into a celebration of another loved one's survival. Photo by Karen Bell

Gallery 2

MAGICICADA SEPTEMDECIM

Michael Godfrey, Charlotte, NC
44" x 66"

Fascinated by cicadas since childhood, Michael incorporated appliqué, embroidery, and hand quilting in his homage to past summers.

POSH

Debbie Bowles, Burnsville, MN
42" x 42", machine quilted by
Brenda Leino

Debbie designed and pieced
this graphic gem of a quilt for
her Maple Island Quilts pattern
company.

SHE'S SO VAIN

Dottie Gantt, Leesville, SC
42" x 62"

Free-motion machine-embroidered
birds were layered and quilted to
create this original view of life in
the jungle.

MAPLE TREES

Priscilla Evans Hair, Easley, NC
48" x 50"

With warm fall colors set against dark batik fabrics, Priscilla used a traditional pieced Leaf block to create this gorgeous swirl of leaves.

DOOR #3: ANGER

Jan Bode Smiley
38" x 77"

Hand-painted and batik fabrics
combine with screen-printed
commercial fabrics to create
this jarring door.

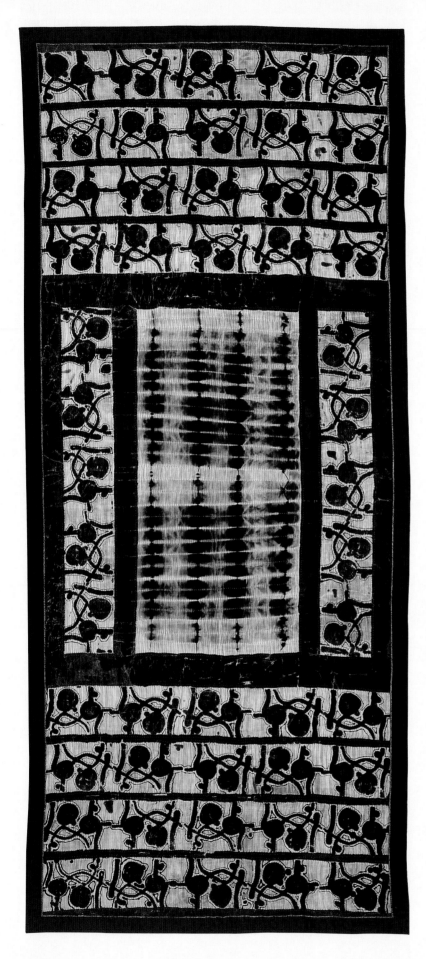

HELLO DARKNESS

Susan Webb Lee, Weddington, NC
37½" x 85"

Black cotton fabric, batiked with a string block, pleated, and discharge-dyed by the artist.

DENPASAR

Jan Bode Smiley
39" x 39"

The warm cinnamon-, saffron-, and curry-toned batiks in this quilt
are from traditional sarongs, purchased on the streets of Denpasar,
the capital of Bali, Indonesia. I combined them with contemporary
batiks, screen prints, and yarn-dyed woven fabrics in irregular Nine-
Patch blocks to create this reminder of Bali's sights and smells.

DARK JUNGLE

Paula H. Brown, Aiken, SC
58" x 33"
Tiger faces and many other jungle-inspired batik patterns
combine in this wonderfully original quilt.

Back

LOOKING BACK...
GHOST IN THE DESERT ROCK

Patricia L. Styring, Jacksonville, FL
60" x 71"

A carved giraffe in a North African desert rock inspired Patricia to craft this original quilt. After drawing her own version of the giraffes, she combined handmade stamps, bleach discharge, a plethora of batik fabrics, and her wonderful sense of design to create both the front and back art.

Front

STAMP OUT DECAF

Jan Bode Smiley
35" x 27"

Strips of soft batiks surround hand-stamped coffee and tea images.

I-RIS-K NOTHING

Joanne Westphal, Chapin, SC
55½" x 62½"

Joanne created this incredible iris quilt inspired
by Ruth McDowell's *Pieced Flowers* book.

GOING DUTCH

Claire Tinsley, South Yorkshire, England
42" x 58"

Inspired by Amsterdam's flower and vegetable markets, Claire used acrylic paints on commercial cottons. She masterfully layered the shapes, quilted around them, and then cut away the top layer to expose the batik background.

DOOR STUDY #3:
BEHIND CLOSED DOORS

Jan Bode Smiley
22" x 24"
Raw-edge strips were layered
onto batting and backing and then
heavily machine quilted for texture.

SUMMER SQUASH

Jan Bode Smiley
55" x 54"

Many green and yellow batiks, and
hand-dyed and yarn-dyed woven
fabrics were sewn together in strips
to create a large piece of cloth.
From this cloth, I cut squares and
set them on point. Meandering
machine quilting completes the
project. This is a great opportunity
to use up bits and pieces of strips
left over from other projects.

LOOS FAMILY QUILT

Sally M. Loos, Agawam, MA
35" x 43"

Sally used cotton batiks to create the perfect safe place for hundreds of representational objects.

ROOT CELLAR

Susan Brittingham, Riner, VA
67" x 68"

This pictorial quilt was Susan's response to a group challenge to create a quilt illustrating tranquility.

Quilting Basics

Fabric requirements are calculated on a 42"-width; many fabrics shrink when washed, and widths vary by manufacturer and country of origin. When cutting, unless otherwise specified, cut strips on the crosswise grain.

Prewashing

If you plan to wash a finished quilt, prewashing your fabrics is recommended. If you have no intention of washing the finished quilt, prewashing is optional. Keep in mind that fabrics do tend to shrink at different rates.

When prewashing batik and hand-dyed fabrics, don't panic if you see some excess dye in the water. Frequently there is some leftover dye that will rinse off. Most often, this dye is exhausted and cannot attach itself to other fibers. To be on the safe side, prewash like colors together, and buy your fabrics from a reputable source.

To test whether the excess dye is exhausted, wash the fabric in question with a clean light-colored washcloth. If the washcloth color is not affected by the fabric, you don't need to worry that the dye will attach itself to another fabric in your finished project.

General Guidelines

Seam Allowances

A ¼" seam allowance is used for most projects. It is recommended that you test your seam allowance before beginning the project to ensure that your ¼" is accurate.

Pressing

In general, press seams toward the darker fabric. Press lightly, using the appropriate temperature for your fabric. Avoid over-ironing, which can distort your fabric.

Borders

When border strips are cut on the crosswise grain, you often need to piece the strips together to achieve the needed lengths. Wider borders typically look better if the seams are sewn on the diagonal.

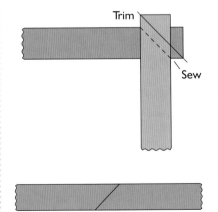

Butted Borders

In most cases the side borders are sewn on first. When you have finished the quilt top, measure through the center vertically. This will be the length to cut the side borders. Place pins at the centers of all four sides of the quilt top, as well as in the center of each side border strip. Pin the side borders to the quilt top, matching the center pins. Using a ¼" seam allowance, sew the borders to the quilt top and carefully press.

Measure horizontally across the center of the quilt top including the side borders. This will be the length to cut the top and bottom borders. Repeat pinning, sewing, and pressing.

Backing

Plan on making the backing a minimum of 2" larger than the quilt top on all sides. Prewash the fabric, and trim the selvages before you piece.

To economize, you can piece the back from leftover fabrics or blocks in your collection. The backs of quilts can be a great place to use up pieces of fabrics that are no longer your favorites. Going one step further, here's an opportunity to use an unfinished project about which you've been feeling guilty!

Batting

The type of batting to use is a personal decision based on many factors. Is your quilt traditional or contemporary? Do you want the batting to shrink after you have finished your quilt? How large is your quilt? How much can you afford to spend on batting? Have you used extremely dark or very light fabrics in your quilt top? All of these factors should be considered. Consult your local quilt shop for assistance. Cut batting approximately 2" larger on all sides than your quilt top.

Layering

Spread the backing wrong side up and tape the edges down with masking tape. (If you are working on carpet you can use T-pins to secure the backing to the carpet.) Center the batting on top, taking care to smooth out any folds. Place the quilt top right side up on top, centering it on the batting and backing.

Basting

If you plan to machine quilt, pin-baste the quilt layers together with safety pins placed a minimum of 3"–4" apart. Begin basting in the center and move toward the edges first in vertical, then horizontal rows. You can also use basting spray to layer the quilt; be sure to follow the manufacturer's instructions.

If you plan to hand quilt, baste the layers together with thread using a long needle and light-colored thread. Knot one end of the thread. Using stitches approximately the length of the needle, begin in the center and move out toward the edges.

Quilting

Quilting by hand, machine, or a combination of techniques should enhance the pieced or appliquéd design of the quilt. You may choose to quilt in-the-ditch, echo the pieced or appliquéd motifs, use patterns from quilting design books and stencils, or do your own free-motion quilting.

Binding

Double-Fold Straight-Grain Binding (French Fold)

Trim excess batting and backing from the quilt. If you want a ½" finished binding, cut the strips 2¾" wide and piece together with a diagonal seam to make a continuous binding strip.

Press the seams open, then carefully press the entire strip in half lengthwise with wrong sides together. With raw edges even, pin the binding to the edge of the quilt a few inches away from the corner, and leave the first few inches of the binding unattached. Start sewing, using a ½" seam allowance.

Stop ½" away from the first corner (see Step 1) and backstitch one stitch. Lift the presser foot and needle. Rotate the quilt one-quarter turn. Fold the binding at a right angle so it extends straight above the quilt (see Step 2). Then bring the binding strip down even with the edge of the quilt (see Step 3). Begin sewing at the folded edge.

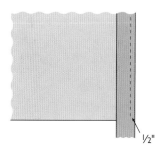

½"

Step 1. Stitch to ½" from corner.

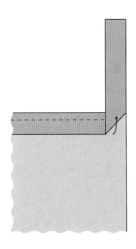

Step 2. First fold for miter

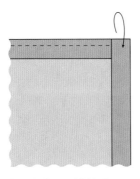

Step 3. Second fold alignment
Repeat in the same manner at all corners.

Finishing the Binding

I join the last seam on the bias to reduce bulk just as the other seams. Fold the binding over the raw edges to the quilt back and hand stitch, mitering the corners.

Machine Appliqué Using Fusible Web

Lay the fusible web sheet paper-side-up on the pattern, and trace with a pencil. Trace detail lines with a permanent marker for ease in transferring to the fabric.

Following the manufacturer's instructions, fuse the web patterns to the wrong side of the appliqué fabric. It helps to use an appliqué-pressing sheet to avoid getting the adhesive on your iron or ironing board.

Cut out the pieces along the pencil line. Remove the paper and position the appliqué piece on your project. Be sure the web (rough) side is down. Press in place, following the manufacturer's instructions.

Paper Piecing

Sew on the side of the paper with the printed lines; the fabric is placed on the non-printed side.

Note: With paper piecing you don't have to worry about the grain of the fabric. You are stitching on paper and that stabilizes the block. The paper is not torn off until after the blocks are stitched together.

1. Trace or photocopy the number of paper-piecing patterns you need for your project.

2. Use a smaller-than-usual stitch length (#1.5–1.8 or 18 to 20 stitches per inch), and a slightly larger needle (size 90/14). This stitch length makes the paper removal easier, and will result in tighter stitches that can't be pulled apart when you tear the paper off.

3. Cut the pieces slightly larger than necessary—about ¾" larger; they do not need to be perfect shapes. (One of the joys of paper piecing!)

4. Follow the number sequence (if given) when piecing. Pin piece #1 in place on the blank side of the paper, but make sure you don't place the pin anywhere near a seam line. Hold the paper up to the light to be sure the piece covers the area it is supposed to, with the seam allowance also amply covered.

5. Fold the pattern back at the stitching line, and trim the fabric to a ¼" seam allowance with a ruler and rotary cutter.

6. Cut piece #2 large enough to cover the area of #2, plus a generous seam allowance. It's a good idea to cut each piece larger than you think necessary; it might be a bit wasteful, but is easier than ripping out tiny stitches! Align the edge with the trimmed seam allowance of piece #1, right sides together, and pin. Paper side up, stitch one line.

7. Open piece #2 and press.

8. Continue stitching each piece in order, being sure to fold back the paper pattern and trim the seam allowance to ¼" before adding the next piece.

9. Trim all around the finished unit to the ¼" seam allowance. Leave the paper intact until after the blocks have been sewn together, then carefully remove the paper. Creasing the paper at the seamline helps when tearing it.

Contributors List

Many thanks to the following companies for their contributions to the success of this book.

Batiks Etcetera & Sew What Fabrics
460 E. Main Street
Wytheville, VA 24382
800.228.4573
www.batiks.com
Incredible selection of batik fabrics
Secure online ordering and
mail order

Batik World, LLC
5006 Shenandoah Lane Place
Baton Rouge, Louisiana 70817
225.755.7466
www.BatikWorld.com
Traditional Malaysian batiks

Bold Over Batiks!
458 Warwick Street
St. Paul MN 55105
888.830.7455
www.boldoverbatiks.com
Malaysian batik fabrics

Dharma Trading Co.
P.O. Box 150916
San Rafael, CA 94915
800.542.5227
www.dharmatrading.com
Dye supplies

Hoffman California Fabrics
25792 Obrero Drive
Mission Viejo, CA 92691
800.547.0100
www.hoffmanfabrics.com
Bali batik fabrics

Island Batik, Inc.
1341 Distribution Way #12
Vista, CA 92081
888.522.2845
www.islandbatik.com
Indonesia batik fabrics and paintings

Kent Avery
1375 Broadway
New York, NY 10018
212.354.7400
Nancy Crow-designed fabrics

P&B Textiles
1580 Gilbreth Road
Burlingame, CA 94010
800.852.2327
www.pbtex.com
Plaids and stripes

Princess Mirah Design
from Bali Fabrics, Inc.
554 Third Street West
Sonoma, CA 95476
800.783.4612
www.balifab.com
Balinese batik fabrics

Quilters Dream Batting
589 Central Drive
Virginia Beach, VA 23454
888.268.8664
www.quiltersdreambatting.com

Timeless Treasures
483 Broadway
New York, NY 10013
212.226.1400
www.ttfabrics.com
Batik and yarn-dyed fabrics

YLI Corporation
161 W. Main St.
Rock Hill, SC 29730
800.296.8139
www.ylicorp.com
Cotton, silk, and synthetic threads

About the Author

Jan grew up in the Midwest with a mom who bakes and knits, a dad who loved to build things, a grandma who sewed clothing, and another grandma who canned anything within reach. Although none of them were quiltmakers, their aptitude for making things definitely influenced Jan.

Jan made her first quilt block, based on a magazine photo, when she was a teenager. She began to quilt in earnest years later, when pregnant with her first child. She quickly gravitated toward contemporary quilts based on traditional designs. Her work has been exhibited nationally, and she has been teaching and lecturing since the late 80s.

Jan's passion for batik fabrics led her to found Batiks Etcetera, a mail-order source for batik fabrics from around the world. After selling the business, she went back to her studio, where she happily spends as much time as possible.

Photo by Tom Smiley

Index